Guess What Happened at School Today

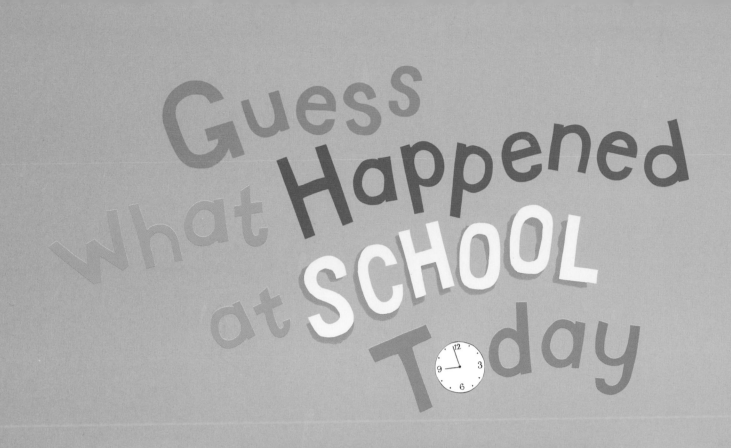

Poor Dan Davies
(how uncool)
forgot he was in
class at school.
Picked his nose,
sucked his thumb
and by mistake
he called Miss
'Mum!'

Jez Alborough

for
Cecily

First published in hardback in Great Britain by
HarperCollins Publishers Ltd in 2003

1 3 5 7 9 10 8 6 4 2
ISBN: 0-00-713630-7

Text and illustrations copyright © Jez Alborough 2003
Designed by Ian Butterworth
The author/illustrator asserts the moral right to be identified as the
author/illustrator of the work.
A CIP catalogue record for this title is available from the British Library.
All rights reserved. No part of this publication may be reproduced, stored
in a retrieval system or transmitted in any form or by any means,
electronic, mechanical, photocopying, recording or otherwise, without the
prior permission of HarperCollins Publishers Ltd, 77-85 Fulham Palace Road,
Hammersmith, London W6 8JB.
The HarperCollins website address is: www.fireandwater.com
Printed and bound in China

Special thanks to
Gail Penston and
Graham Alborough

With thanks to
Thomas's Preparatory School, Battersea, London
and Maltman's Green School,
Gerrards Cross, Bucks.

TIMETABLE

	The One Who Comes in Late
ASSEMBLY	Morning Prayer
MATHS	That Thing That You Said
ENGLISH	Are You Supposed to be Somewhere?
BREAK	Teacher Playtime
	Miss Chadwick's in a Mood Today
	Don't Lean Back On Your Chair, Claire
I.T.	Chatterbox
P.E.	The Human Zoo
LUNCH	Rosie's Rabbit's Run Away
LUNCH BREAK	Joanna's Got a Horse Called Ned
	Nigel's Knee
SCIENCE	Our Tree
	My Class
ART	Ten Minutes to Go
STORYTIME	Teacher Out of School
HOME TIME	Guess What Happened at School Today

9 x 3 =

Collins

An imprint of HarperCollinsPublishers

The One Who Comes in Late

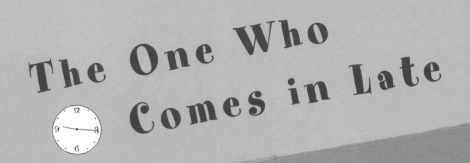

The streets are clear of parents' cars,
all except for one car – ours.
It's nine o'clock and time for school,
time to be there – that's the rule.
The bell is ringing, but *I* can't hear it,
because I'm sat here, nowhere near it.

We pull up right beside the gate –
we're the only car that's late.
Today we've got Assembly –
they're all in there, except for me.
A quick goodbye, then off I rush,
panting through the playground's hush.

I can hear a distant telephone
and our headteacher's muffled drone.
Then from the office, sipping tea,
the secretary beckons me.

In wheezing whispers I explain
why I'm stood here – late again.
She points across the polished floors
that lead towards the big oak doors.

Peering out through steamed-up glasses
I tiptoe slow past empty classes.
Our headteacher's voice gets stronger.
I wish the corridor was longer.

Feeling really, really small,
I stop outside the dreaded hall.
It's nine-fifteen – oh, how I hate

to be the one

who comes

in late.

Morning Prayer

Our headteacher thinks it's best
to end Assembly with a test.
We sit there on bony bums,
he just points and calls out sums.

As he rises from his chair,
each day I say my morning prayer.
I close my eyes and mouth each word
and hope my morning prayer is heard.

*O**ur headteacher – please be kind
if this crouching boy you find.
Ask the question clear and slow,
keep thy numbers nice and low,
or better still, point o'er this head
and pick on someone else instead.*

He stalks around the silent hall,
we wonder where his gaze will fall.
He works his way towards our class,
we sway away like windswept grass.

RICHARD DRIVER – NINE TIMES THREE?
Please Mr Rimmington, don't pick me!

Just like a heron hunting fishes,
eyeballs open wide like dishes.
His head keeps twitching left and right,
I try to stay just out of sight.

CLAIRE TOOGOOD – TWELVE TIMES THREE?
Please Mr Rimmington, don't pick me!

Claire's not scared – Claire's so smart
she knows the answers off by heart.
She sits up straight and almost glows
with all the answers that she knows.

EIGHT TIMES THREE – JAMES McNEE?
Please Mr Rimmington, don't pick me!

Crouching low behind our Claire,
hope he doesn't spot me there.
Hold my breath, make no sound.
Stay there Claire – don't turn around.

NOW LET ME SEE – NINE TIMES THREE –
WHO WILL ANSWER THIS FOR ME?
WHO'S THAT SKULKING ROUND DOWN THERE,
HIDING RIGHT BEHIND OUR CLAIRE?

What happened next is somewhat blurred
but Nigel told me that he heard:
'Please Sir, it's *er* ... only me.
Is the answer ... twenty-three?'

TWENTY-THREE? NO, NO, GOOD HEAVENS,
NINE TIMES THREE IS TWENTY-SEVEN!

I promised next time I'd be able
to run through all the three times table.
But I know this boy will still be there,
head bowed, eyes closed in morning prayer.

That Thing That You Said

It came out of nowhere – like a runaway ball,
    that thing that you said at the back of the hall.
It caught me off guard, smack in the belly
    and I laughed 'til I quivered and shivered like jelly.

There wouldn't have been a problem at all
    if I'd finished my giggle back in the hall.
But now we're in class and I'm starting to dread
    the giggle coming back with that thing that you said.

I'm being quite stern, with a serious frown.
    I'm holding the tickle inside of me down.
It's jumping and bumping and trying to get free.
    Oh, why did you have to sit right next to me?

You scribbled a note on the back of your book,
    I knew what it was but I still had to look...
Now a pinball is bouncing around in my head –
    it's etched with the words of that thing that you said.

There's a damp patch of sweat
on the back of my shirt,
there are cramps in my ribs
which are starting to hurt.
The desk top is quaking,
the pencils are shaking
in time with the rhythm
my shoulders are making.
I'm writhing and squirming,
my face is bright red —
but I'm *not* going to laugh
at that thing that you said.

I'll think about how at the end of the day,
I can laugh 'til the giggle's all giggled away.
By tonight I'll forget what was funny at all
'bout that thing that you said at the back of the hall.
That thing that I'm not even thinking about,
though the lump in my throat is trying to get out.
I'll hold my breath, I'll burst instead,
but *I'm* not, *I'm not, I'm not* going to laugh
at that thing that you said!

Are You Supposed to be Somewhere?

Along the corridor he passes,
squinting in on busy classes.
The bell has gone – it's half past ten,
Adam Gage is lost again.

He's searching in the usual places,
trying to spot familiar faces
belonging to the class he's in –
the class he's mislaid once again.

Miss Chadwick calls out from her chair:
'Are you supposed to be somewhere?'
Adam nods and says, *'Yes, Miss.*
But I don't know where that somewhere is.
I came out of Assembly
and forgot where I was meant to be.
I'm in Class Eight – beside the stairs –
there's nothing there but empty chairs.'

So Miss says, *'Well, they can't be far –*
Timetables tell us where we are.
Take yours out – and use your eyes.'
'I can't, I've lost it!' Adam cries.

'Miss!' cries Anne, with arm up straight,
'My brother, John, is in Class Eight.
Tuesday morning's their P.E.,
each week right after 'sembly.'

Miss Chadwick says, *'Well, now we know.*
They're in the hall – so off you go
and, Adam, let this be a warning,
don't come back next Tuesday morning.'

So Adam leaves, we wait, and then –
right on cue – he's back again.
'Miss,' he says, *'I know I'm near, but...*
which way is the hall from here?'

Teacher Playtime

Imagine if at break today
the teachers all went out to play
while, in the staff room, children sat,
sipping tea and swapping chat.

What would the grown ups do d'you think,
without their chat and tea to drink?
How would all our teachers be,
in the playground, running free?
Why don't you come along with me
on playground duty – then we'll see?

Miss Colgate skips with Miss McPhinn,
Miss Chadwick asks, *'Can I join in?'*
'Go on,' I say, *'she's on her own.'*
'Do we have to, Sir?' the teachers groan.

Our headteacher climbs a tree
and shouts, *'Hey, you lot – look at me!'*
'You're not supposed to be up there!'
'So what?' he hollers. *'I don't care!'*

Miss Sykes hangs from the climbing frame
and calls the head a naughty name.
'Now that's not very nice!' I cry.
'He said it first,' comes her reply.

Mr Philips, in his gym,
pretends a crowd is watching him.
He swings his bat at phantom balls,
then proudly laps the empty hall.

Who's that kissing Mr Day?
'Enough of that, Miss Cook!' I say.
'I'm going to keep my eye on you,
now go find something else to do.'

Imagine if at break today
the teachers all went out to play.
By the time we heard the bell
there'd be so many tales to tell.
And when they'd all come in from play,
if we were bad in class, I'd say,
'Don't tell us off or make a fuss,
we know you're just as bad as us.'

Miss Chadwick's in a Mood Today

Beware when you come in from play,
    Miss Chadwick's in a mood today.
Take a little tip from me,
    be quieter than you'd like to be.
Keep your idle chit-chat canned,
    when asking questions, raise your hand.
Don't slouch or slump or tap your feet,
    make your writing nice and neat.

Be good when you come in from play,
    Miss Chadwick's in a mood today.
Don't let her catch you pulling faces,
    put books back in their proper places.
If she pops out to the corridor,
    be as quiet as you were before.
Work hard and, for goodness sake,
    don't make her late for morning break.

What's the matter, who can tell?
Is she just not feeling well?
Has her cat just passed away?
Was the traffic worse today?
Is someone parking in her space?
Could that explain her furrowed face?

Is she under too much strain?
Has her diet gone down the drain?
Has she heard some nasty news?
Did she step in doggy-doos?
Has she had a sleepless night?
Are her underpants too tight?
Does she need a great big cry?
We just don't know the reason why.

But please take heed of what I say,
don't mess around in class today.
Be good 'til you go out to play,
Miss Chadwick's in a mood today.

Don't Lean Back On Your Chair, Claire!

Don't lean back on your chair, Claire!
Don't lean back on your chair.
Use all four legs that are there, Claire,
don't lean back on your chair!

Don't lean back on your chair, Claire!
You really must sit with more care.
If you fall you'll have quite a scare, Claire,
so don't lean back on your chair.

Don't lean back on your chair, Claire!
You're displaying your underwear.
Stop rocking about in the air, Claire,
don't lean back on your...!

Pick up your three-legged chair, Claire!
Pick up your three-legged chair.
Bring it up here for repair, Claire,
then sit at the back over there.

Don't tell me it's unfair, Claire!
I told you to take some more care.
Sit there and don't you *dare*, Claire...
Don't lean back
on your
chair!

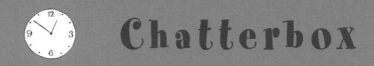

Chatterbox

Chinwag, yak, blab,
chitter-chat-chatter.
Pow-wow, how-now,
have a good natter.

Yackety-yak, answer back,
jibby-jaw, prattle.
Rabbit-rabbit, blah blah,
a little tittle-tattle.

Squawk, talk, gush, gas,
blab, gob, gabble.
Yap, rap, jive, bleat,
warble, burble, babble.

We all possess a voice box –
Miss Chadwick said we did.
The trouble is some people never
want to close

the lid.

The Human Zoo

We grab a tray, grab a plate,
grab a bite to eat.
We grab a knife, a fork and spoon,
a table and a seat.

Rudi eats without a word,
Nancy pecks just like a bird,
Milly chews with jaw ajar
and hums just like a racing car.

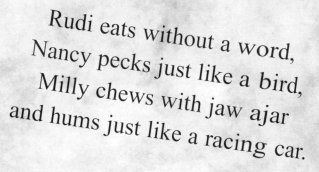

Sanjay gobbles very fast,
Elaine makes every mouthful last,
Trevor takes his plate and stirs,
while Ida holds on tight to hers.

Gail drops drips and spots her dress,
Barry makes an awful mess
that Ida steps in on the floor
when she goes up to get some more.

Nigel gulps, Rosita sips,
Russell always licks his lips,
Jenny dribbles, Yemi slurps,
and, when he's finished, Barry burps.

Every day from one 'til two
the hall becomes a human zoo.
It's a feeding frenzy, free for all,
at dinner time – down in our hall.

Rosie's Rabbit's Run Away

Rosie's rabbit's run away,
that's why Rosie cried at play.
The hutch he lived in was no good –
Nibbles nibbled through the wood.

His breakfast bowl had been upset,
his fresh straw bed was soaking wet.
He'd made a mess with all his stuff
as if he'd hopped off in a huff.

There's one thing we all want to know –
where did Rosie's Nibbles go?
Rosie said she thought she knew –
the dew-damp grass had left a clue.

Hop prints formed a trail which led
towards the gate, behind the shed.
Now Nibbles nibbles on his own
in the big wide world alone.
No more meals brought to his door –
a menu from the forest floor.

Rosie's rabbit's run away,
that's why Rosie cried at play.

Joanna's Got a Horse Called Ned

Joanna's got a horse called Ned –
a chestnut-coloured thoroughbred.
And everywhere Joanna goes,
she makes sure everybody knows.
We've heard it all ten times before
but every play she brags some more.

Joanna's got a horse called Ned –
they jump in shows at Maidenhead.
She trains each day right after school –
Joanna thinks she's really cool.
She said she'd bring in her rosettes
but somehow always just forgets.

Joanna's got a horse called Ned –
at least that's what Joanna said,
but no one's seen Joanna's horse
because it isn't real, of course.
Joanna's got a horse called Ned –
it lives inside Joanna's head.

Nigel's Knee

Nigel's bashed and gashed his knee –
  a small crowd gathers round to see.
He hit the tarmac, you can tell,
  a red spot marks where Nigel fell.
He's near to tears, with glassy eyes,
  bunched up on his side, he lies.

  Miss Chadwick, on her walkabout,
    strolls across to sort things out.
'He fell down there and hurt his knee.
    He's crying, Miss,' bleats Ann Marie.
Nigel looks the other way.
    'No, I'm not,' he wants to say,
but keeps his purple lips pressed tight.
    Otherwise he knows he might.

    The lunchtime bell's already gone –
      Miss crouches down, the crowd looks on.
She bends the knee so tenderly –
    down Nigel's cheek, a tear breaks free.
The children stare – no words are spoken
      'til Miss announces, *'Nothing broken.'*
    She smiles and nudges Nigel's chin
      and Nigel grins a tearful grin.

Miss scans the crowd – who will it be?
　　Each earnest face shouts, 'Please pick me!'
'*Anne,*' she says, '*and ... yes, Louise,*
　　take Nigel to the Office, please.
The rest of you, school's begun.'
　　The children softly moan as one.

　　　　Miss Chadwick shepherds them away,
　　　　　　Louise and Anne are still at play.
　　　　With hands held, grinning, off they stride,
　　　　　　with Nigel hobbling by their side.

　　　　Exploring empty corridors,
　　　　　　their shoes squeak on the polished floors.
　　　　Kids stare from lessons as they pass
　　　　　　and wonder why they're not in class.
　　　　The girls keep marching straight ahead
　　　　　　but giggle every time they tread.
　　　　The last thing on their fizzed-up minds
　　　　　　is Nigel limping just behind.

　　　　He doesn't care, his leg is sore
　　　　　　but it doesn't sting much anymore.
　　　　Now all that hurts is Nigel's pride –
　　　　　　he wishes that he hadn't cried,
　　　　but hopes there'll be a scar to see,
　　　　　　to mark the day
　　　　　　he bashed his knee.

Our Tree

In Science Class at school today,
  Miss said, *'Put your books away,'*
then led us quietly, hand-in-hand,
  outside to where the oak tree stands.

In the shade beneath the tree
  she told us how it came to be.
'An acorn fell here long ago,
  the sun shone down and made it grow.
Downwards reached a spreading root
  and upwards pushed a tiny shoot.

It sprouted spring leaves here and there
  which caught the light and breathed the air.
It drank the rain and morning dew,
  it fed on earth and slowly grew.
Many summers passed this way
  to make the tree we see today.'

Just then a nearby puddle plopped.
    'Look!' I cried. *'An acorn's dropped.'*
Miss picked it up, we looked around
    and found a sunlit patch of ground.
We dug a hole, placed it in
    and let the story of our tree begin.

We pointed where our acorn lay.
    Miss took a snap to mark the day
so all our mums and dads will see
    how we helped to plant our tree.

When it grows up   tall and strong,
    I hope a teacher comes along
and brings her class so they can see
    how Mother Nature grows a tree.

She'll show our photograph and say,
    'This tree began that autumn day.'
And when they know how trees are grown,
    perhaps they'll plant one of their own.

My Class

Even if you are
one of a twin,
we're all of us different –
outside and in.

Paul's really tall
and **Noah** is lower.
It's not his fault,
he just grows a bit slower.

Brenda is slender,
Ida looks wider –
especially when Brenda
sits down beside her.

Russell's got muscles
and so has our **Jenny**.
Tony is bony –
he hasn't got any.

Dale can look pale –
just like margarine.
Mark is quite dark
and **Dean**'s in-between.

Cliff is so stiff –
have you seen how he sits?
Wendy is bendy –
she can still do the splits.

Nick is just quick –
he's bright and he's breezy.
But **Joe**, he goes slow,
n-i-c-e a-n-d e-a-s-y.

Milly is silly
while **Brad** is quite mad.
Miles often smiles
but somehow seems sad.

Rudi is moody,
he's broody and sour.
Pete is just sweet
like a delicate flower.

Trevor is clever,
his head's in the air.
Wayne's got a brain
but forgets that it's there.

You're not me
and I'm not you.
I don't look
the way you do.
If the difference between us
just wasn't there,
there'd be nothing to get
and nothing to share.
So, let's celebrate
the way that we grew –
what makes me, me
and what makes you, you.
You is all you've got to be
and all I've got to be
is me.

Ten Minutes to Go

It's time to go home – it's time to go play,
everyone here's had enough for today.
The hamster is curled up, asleep in his straw,
we can hardly keep awake anymore.

Now every so often Miss Chadwick sighs,
she's developed that faraway look in her eyes.
Ten minutes to go and her battery's low
so she slumps and she slouches and speaks rather slow.

Sometimes she trails off a sentence midway –
forgets what it was she was going to say.
We look up like puppets with empty-eye stares,
no one was listening – nobody cares.

A bird in the playground is hopping around,
pecking a packet of crisps that it's found.
There's a glove on the wall and a ball by the drain,
just waiting for someone to kick it again.

The last of the afternoon sunlight has gone,
the dark is descending, the street lamps are on.
Some parents are already down at the gate,
chatting on phones to their friends while they wait.

Everyone knows that time passes slow
when you wait for the 'time-to-go-home' bell to go.
So I wait and I wait -- then I get quite a shock:
It's the bell, and it yells:

'IT'S GO HOME O'CLOCK!'

Teacher Out of School

Out shopping after school with Dad, just after half past four,
    walking through the supermarket, who do you think I saw?
'It's Miss!' I whispered in Dad's ear.
    'Miss who?' he said. *'Don't stare.'*
'Miss Chadwick, from our school!' I cried. *'She's standing over there!'*

I wished myself invisible, I wished to be elsewhere –
    in our shed, beneath my bed – just somewhere else but there.
A teacher spotted outside school's a most disturbing sight.
    A teacher needs us children and a classroom to look right.

Dad dragged me off towards her (he wouldn't let me run),
    then calmly introduced himself and said I was his son.
    She shook his hand and chatted, just like other adults do,
    and I noticed in her basket was a cake that we have too!

She wasn't like a teacher, I know it sounds quite dumb –
    she looked more like an auntie or someone else's mum.
'Must get back to feed the cat,' she said (I tried to smile),
    then she picked a yoghurt from the shelf
and set off down the aisle.

How stomach churning, foot squirming,
    embarrassingly bad,
to have Miss Chadwick see me there,
    out shopping with my dad.

Watch out on the High Street, be wary in a crowd,
    there are teachers prowling outside school – it shouldn't be allowed.
Teachers should be kept in school, that's where they're meant to be,
    not pretending to be normal people – just like you or me.

Guess What Happened at School Today

When I get home to Mum I'll say,
'Guess what happened at school today?'
And then in words I'll paint a scene
of all the things today has been.

The things I shared, the things I hid,
things I didn't, things I did.
Things I should have, things I shouldn't.
Things I wanted to, but couldn't.

Things I've thought, things I've seen,
things I've said but didn't mean.
Things I've felt but didn't say –
there's so many things that happened today.

I just can't stop when I begin –
it's hard to fit the whole day in.
It's like a game we like to play
called 'Guess What Happened at School Today'.